TASTE and SEE

ALSO BY MARGARET FEINBERG

Scouting the Divine: My Search for God in Wine, Wool, and Wild Honey (Book and Bible Study)

Hungry for God: Discovering God's Voice in the Ordinary and Everyday

Wonderstruck: Awaken to the Nearness of God (Book and Bible Study)

Fight Back with Joy: Celebrate More. Regret Less. Stare Down Your Greatest Fears. (Book and Bible Study)

Pursuing God (Study Guide and Video)

TASTE and SEE

Discovering God Among Butchers,
Bakers, & Fresh Food Makers

BIBLE STUDY GUIDE | SIX SESSIONS

MARGARET FEINBERG

ZONDERVAN

Taste and See Bible Study Guide
Copyright © 2018 by Margaret Feinberg

This title is also available as a Zondervan ebook.

Requests for information should be addressed to:
Zondervan, 3900 Sparks Dr. SE, Grand Rapids, Michigan 49546

ISBN 978-0-310-08781-6

All Scripture quotations, unless otherwise noted, are taken from the Holy Bible, New International Version®, NIV®. Copyright © 1973, 1978, 1984, 2011 by Biblica, Inc.® Used by permission of Zondervan. All rights reserved worldwide. www.Zondervan.com. The "NIV" and "New International Version" are trademarks registered in the United States Patent and Trademark Office by Biblica, Inc.®

Scripture quotations marked ESV are taken from the ESV® Bible (The Holy Bible, English Standard Version®). Copyright © 2001 by Crossway, a publishing ministry of Good News Publishers. Used by permission. All rights reserved.

Scripture quotations marked NASB are taken from the New American Standard Bible®. Copyright © 1960, 1962, 1963, 1968, 1971, 1972, 1973, 1975, 1977, 1995 by The Lockman Foundation. Used by permission. (www.Lockman.org).

Any internet addresses (websites, blogs, etc.) and telephone numbers in this book are offered as a resource. They are not intended in any way to be or imply an endorsement by Zondervan, nor does Zondervan vouch for the content of these sites and numbers for the life of this book.

All rights reserved. No part of this publication may be reproduced, stored in a retrieval system, or transmitted in any form or by any means—electronic, mechanical, photocopy, recording, or any other—except for brief quotations in printed reviews, without the prior permission of the publisher.

Author is represented by Christopher Ferebee, Attorney and Literary Agent, www.christopherferebee.com.

Cover design: Faceout Studio
Cover photography: Shutterstock / Stocksy
Interior design: Denise Froehlich

First printing October 2018 / Printed in the United States of America

Meet the Author 7
Dear Leader 9
Leader's Guide 11

SESSION 1: You're Invited to the Table 15
SESSION 2: Delighting in the Sweetness of Fruitfulness 37
SESSION 3: Chewing on the Bread of Life 55
SESSION 4: Savoring the Salt of the Earth 75
SESSION 5: Relishing the Olive and Its Oil 97
SESSION 6: Discovering the Liturgy of the Table 115

Taste and See Memorization Flash Cards 123
Recipe Index 127
Notes 133
Free Gifts 135

Meet the Author

Margaret Feinberg is a popular Bible teacher and speaker at churches and leading conferences such as Catalyst and Women of Joy. Her books and Bible studies, including *Scouting the Divine*, *Fight Back with Joy*, *Wonderstruck*, and *The Sacred Echo*, have sold more than a million copies and received critical acclaim and extensive national media coverage from CNN, the Associated Press, *USA Today*, the *Los Angeles Times*, the *Washington Post*, and many others.

She was named one of the 50 women most shaping culture and the church today by *Christianity Today*. Margaret lives in Park City, Utah, with her husband Leif who serves as a local pastor, and their superpup, Hershey.

Now that you've read the official bio, here's the kick-off-your-shoes-and-drink-iced-tea-on-the-back-porch version:

Margaret spends most mornings with her good friends, Coffee and God. Without coffee, mornings would be difficult. Without God, life would be impossible.

You'll often find Margaret (puppy-in-tow) adventuring outdoors—she enjoys hiking, river rafting, and scanning the night sky for the Northern Lights and shooting stars.

She boasts an exceptionally dry sense of humor that she attributes to her Jewish father. Little known secret: He was recently inducted into the Surfer's Hall of Fame, and her mom earned her captain's license for sixty-ton ships.

Married to Leif for more than a decade, Margaret's known for losing things like her sunglasses on her head, keys in her hand, and her phone for the twelfth time in the same day. Always up for an adventure, Margaret is known to drive fifty miles to chase down a food truck and snag Groupons for river rafting on a whim. She prefers watching comedies and laughing until her tummy aches over doing sit-ups.

One of her greatest joys is hearing from her readers. Go ahead, find her on Facebook, Twitter, and Instagram (@mafeinberg), or check out her website at margaretfeinberg.com.

Dear Leader,

I am so grateful for you! I wish I were with you right now to give you a huge hug and whisper thank you in your ear—*thank you, thank you, thank you for taking the time to lead participants through this book and Bible study.*

You are busy. Your time is precious and limited. You're pulled in many different directions. Yet here you are willing to step out in faith and courageously serve others, as they grow closer to Christ. Wahoo! I give God thanks for you.

I have a few hopes and prayers for you:

1. Over the upcoming weeks, I pray God will use you to nourish communities with friendship and belonging as people share their lives, their recipes, their love with each other.
2. I pray the content and questions in this study will become a springboard for deeper exploration of the Bible and the goodness of God.
3. I pray the adventures described in the videos and book will spur your group to embark on their own spiritual culinary adventures.
4. I pray that God awakens each person to the rich connection between the Lord's Table and our daily tables.
5. I pray that you will have your eyes opened and spirit filled so that you never read the Bible the same way again.

I've also asked God to overflow your spiritual reservoirs, too. Drop us a note at hello@margaretfeinberg.com and let us know when your group is meeting; we want to pray for you and your participants during this time.

Thank you, friend, for being courageous enough to lead others deeper in their relationship with Jesus. I can't wait to meet you and give you a big hug in person as we feast on the goodness of God together.

Blessings,

Margaret

Leader's Guide

This brief leader's guide is designed to help you take participants through the book and Bible study. As you prepare for this study, go ahead and watch several sessions of the video ahead of time so that you'll have a feel for the study's direction.

You'll want to make sure you and your participants pick up a copy of the *Taste and See* book. Reading the book in advance will prepare you for leading the study and provide you with all kinds of additional insights and background. Some group members may prefer an ebook, audiobook, or paperback version to get the most out of the experience.

As you prepare for each session, here's a basic outline of what to expect:

 HOMEWORK GROUP DISCUSSION

In each session (with the exception of the first) you will lead the group in a review of the homework from the previous week. Encourage participants to share what they're learning and how the Holy Spirit is at work in their lives.

TASTY ACTIVITY

Depending on the amount of time you have to meet together and the resources available, you'll want to engage in the Tasty Activity. You will find this activity on the group page that begins each week. This interactive icebreaker is designed to be a launchpad for group engagement as well as to move people toward the ideas explored in the teaching. Read ahead to the following week's activity to note the supplies needed and how participants may be able to contribute. You should not have to provide all the food on your own. Consider inviting different people to be responsible for gathering the necessary items, cooking a tasty treat, and leading the group through the activity each week. This is a great way to raise up leaders and get more people in on the fun.

PLAY SESSION VIDEO

After you've finished the homework discussion, it's time to play the video. The teaching presentations will range from 18–24 minutes. Encourage participants to jot down notes, questions, and details as they watch the video, using the space provided.

VIDEO DISCUSSION

Dive into the video discussion questions next. Based on the amount of time your group meets, you may need to prayerfully consider which questions are best suited for your group and its needs. Don't feel as though you need to ask every question. Rely on the Holy Spirit for guidance on any additional or follow-up questions that need to be asked as the discussion progresses.

CLOSING PRAYER

Always save time for prayer before you close. Ask the Holy Spirit to open everyone's eyes and hearts to taste and see God's goodness in greater measure.

DISCLAIMERS

I must make a couple of disclaimers before we go further.

Disclaimer # 1: I have been privileged to grow up in an area of the world with many aisles of food inside grocery stores. Billions of people on the planet don't have that privilege. Even in the United States it's estimated that more than thirteen million children live in food-insecure homes, meaning they regularly do not have enough food to eat. To even talk about food and the Bible and know where our next meal is coming from . . . is a privilege.

I never want us to forget that. You'll notice that throughout this Bible study, some of the activities on Day Five of each session will challenge you to collect food, donate food, or become more educated about food scarcity. I've also teamed up with Compassion International, to which I am donating a portion of the proceeds of this Bible study. Not only do they work with local churches around the world to help children have access to education and healthcare, but they also ensure every child enrolled receives a meal each day at the Compassion centers. I'd encourage you or your group to consider sponsoring a child at compassion.com/margaret-feinberg. **Please see the Compassion International page at the back of the study guide.**

Disclaimer #2: I know that food is a source of pain for many of us. I've struggled both with eating disorders and disordered eating throughout my life, and I hope you will be sensitive to those who wrestle with these and other food-related issues as well. Some days I think I am the last person who should be exploring food and the Bible. Yet the more I study, the more I'm convinced that God wants to redeem food just as he is redeeming us.

You're Invited to the Table

GETTING STARTED (10–15 minutes)

 TASTY ACTIVITY: THE IN-A-PINCH MEAL

What you'll need:

- As a leader, select five random food items—either bring them from your home pantry or borrow them from church kitchen (ask permission, if necessary)—and display them at the group session so everyone can see each one.

1. Invite everyone to imagine that it's 6 p.m. and you need to cook a meal that only includes these ingredients and some spices.

2. Discuss the following:

   - Looking at your ingredients, what dish might you create? On a scale of 1–10 (1 = let's order takeout; 10 = let's add to the menu rotation), how much do you think you'll like it?

   - What's your go-to, in-a-pinch meal when you don't have time?

   - How many times a week do you eat your meals with someone else around the table?

 PLAY SESSION 1 VIDEO (18 minutes)

> See the full recipe for honey mustard dressing in the Recipe Index at the back of this study guide.

NOTES

Foodie: One who takes a particular interest in food.

In the Gospels, Jesus is either coming from a meal, going to a meal, or enjoying a meal—when he's not multiplying a meal.

Table time is transformation time.

What did Jesus do with the bread? He took it. He blessed it. He broke it. He gave it.

On the road to Emmaus, they *encountered* Jesus on the road, but they *recognized* him at the table.

Four questions to make deeper connections around any table:

- How did you affect someone's life today?
- How did someone else affect your life today?
- What blessed you most today?
- What did you notice today that helped you recognize an area of your life that still needs healing?

VIDEO DISCUSSION

1. What stood out to you from today's teaching or had the most impact on you? When is the one table time you're going to add to your calendar this week?

2. Read Matthew 18:20 aloud. Margaret describes that many of the miracles Jesus performed and lessons he taught took place around the table. On a scale of 1–10 (1 = hardly expectant; 10 = highly expectant), how expectant are you to experience Jesus' presence when you gather to eat with others? That Jesus will do something extraordinary? Explain.

3. Margaret says, "Table time is transformation time." How have you found this to be true in your own life? Discuss ways you become more intentional about inviting Christ into your table time.

4. Look up the following passages and note who accompanies Jesus during meals: Luke 5:27–32; 7:36–50; 11:37–41; 14:1–6; 22:14–31. How does Jesus challenge notions of hospitality through the "guest list" you just created? How are you challenged to expand your own guest list?

5. Turn in your Bibles to Luke 24:13–35. Take turns reading through the passage, 2–3 verses each. What stands out to you most from this passage?

6. Respond to each of the four questions Margaret raises during the teaching:

   - How did you affect someone's life today?

   - How did someone else affect your life today?

   - What blessed you most today?

   - What did you notice today that helped you recognize an area of your life that still needs healing?

7. If you have time to go deeper, reflect on the following questions based on the four actions found in Luke 24:30:

   - How is Christ *taking* you deeper in your relationship with him?

- How is Christ *blessing* you?

- How is Christ allowing you to be *broken*?

- How is Christ *giving* you, pouring you out, to the world?

BEFORE THE GROUP ENDS . . .

Next session's Tasty Activity is called "A Fun Fruity Tasting." Review the details of the activity on pages 38–39. Ask for three or more volunteers to commit to bring the food and supplies so the cost and responsibility are shared. If your group chooses to skip the activity, you can still engage in the discussion questions.

 CLOSING PRAYER

As you close in prayer, ask:
- God to expand each participant's capacity to taste and see God's goodness.
- The Holy Spirit to increase expectancy for Jesus at every meal.
- That each participant would experience Christ's presence during table time.

Personal Study Time

DAY ONE: GOD—THE HOST WITH THE MOST

It's far too easy to read the story of creation from a safe distance when we first open our Bibles. We forget that a garden is a place of chirping and humming, textures and hues, sweet scents and sharp smells, tangy tastes and sweet bites. The land is abuzz with life and taste and flavor. In the garden, we catch our first sights and tastes of God's goodness.

Read Genesis 1. In the space that follows, make a list of the specific sights and sounds you imagine you'd experience if you took a stroll with God in the cool of the day.

SIGHTS:

SOUNDS:

SMELLS:

TEXTURES:

TASTES:

The Garden of Eden can be translated "garden of pleasure" or "garden of delight." God could have planted humanity in any setting, yet humankind sprouts in a garden amidst orange blossoms and crunchy legumes. Before humans ever practiced hospitality, God practiced it first.

What does the placement of humanity in such a delicious place reveal about . . .

GOD'S CREATIVITY:

GOD'S GENEROSITY:

GOD'S HOSPITALITY:

GOD'S LOVING-KINDNESS:

You're Invited to the Table 25

God gives humanity a specific responsibility within the garden.

Read Genesis 2:15. What were the responsibilities of humankind in the garden?

The garden is the environment God handpicked for Adam and Eve to discover their purpose and place in the world. In tending the land and tasting its fruits, they discover *their* existence within the landscape of *life's* existence. They learn skills of how to care for the earth and care for each other. The very work Adam is called to do opens a pathway for discovery, knowledge, and understanding to experience God's provision and presence more intimately. Through his placement and purpose in the garden, Adam is more fully able to taste and see that the Lord is good.

QUOTABLE: "To live, we must daily break the body and shed the blood of Creation. When we do this knowingly, lovingly, skillfully, reverently, it is a sacrament." –Wendell Berry[1]

Somewhere in the shadows lurks a dark lanky creature who whispers in the woman's ear, *this one nibble is better than all the rest*. With a bite they disobey, and soon the couple is banned from the holy banquet.

Read Genesis 3:17–19 below. Circle every mention of food and eating in the passage.

> To Adam he said, "Because you listened to your wife and ate fruit from the tree about which I commanded you, 'You must not eat from it,' cursed is the ground because of you; through painful toil you will eat

food from it all the days of your life. It will produce thorns and thistles for you, and you will eat the plants of the field. By the sweat of your brow you will eat your food until you return to the ground."

The broken soil results in painful toil, thorns and thistles, and the sweat of the brow, yet embedded in these words God doesn't eliminate the need for food. The cursed ground makes life hard but also makes humanity more dependent on God for the soil and the seasons, the water and the weather.

You will eat food all the days of your life.

You will eat the plants of the field.

You will eat your food until you return to the ground.

How are these statements still true of us today?

Rather than banish, God redeems food in a surprising heavenly twist. Throughout the following generations, the Israelites experience and commemorate God's power, purpose, and rescue through food. They discover community and satisfaction and healing around the table.

When Jesus appears, he reveals himself as foodstuff: the bread of life, the true vine, the one anointed with olive oil, the sacrificial lamb. The Son of God is even described as someone who knocks on the doors of our souls so we'll invite him in for supper. And when this whole shindig reaches its culmination, God handpicks the menu for the best banquet of all time—one that supersedes anything Adam and Eve experienced in Eden.

God loves us so much that he wants to use everything in our lives—even food—to reveal his goodness.

CLOSING PRAYER

Spend time praying that your senses will be heightened to God's goodness. With each passing page and session, ask God to help you discover another facet of his character, feel the soft pinch of his presence, and step back in astonishment of the One who holds everything together.

DAY TWO: READ AND LEARN

Read chapter 1 of the *Taste and See* book, "An Invitation to a Culinary Adventure." Use the space below to note any insights or questions you want to share at the next group session.

Describe your most memorable meal. How does that memory reveal your deeper heart hunger?

Imagine yourself across the table from Margaret and she asks you, "What are you really hungry for?" How would you answer?

Of all the biblical mentions of food in this chapter, which surprised you the most?

In both the Old Testament and New, God sprinkled hundreds of food references like Hansel and Gretel's breadcrumbs. From that first bite in Genesis, the great story of God is stuffed with mentions of food and feasts. Everyday edibles become both a source of sustenance and of sacred symbolism. Food often takes on a spiritual dimension, a physical representation of God's grace and provision. The table doesn't have to be a place of awkwardness or shame, fear or angst, but food can become a way to feed our bellies and satiate our souls. Indeed, food is an expression of God's love made edible.

When have you experienced food as God's love made edible?

DAY THREE: A MILLION THANK YOUS

Eating is holy, but it's also humbling. Food was never meant to be worshiped; if anything, it was meant to reveal we are not gods and we are dependent on God for everything.

QUOTABLE: "Thoughtful eating reminds us that there is no human fellowship without a table, no table without a kitchen, no kitchen without a garden, no garden without viable ecosystems, no ecosystems without the forces productive of life, and no life without its source in God." –Norman Wirzba[2]

The morsels of life that fill our belly remind us that the nourishment of God extends beyond our physical needs to our emotional, relational, and spiritual needs.

If you pray before a meal, what is your common prayer? Write it in the space below.

Reflecting on our source of food reminds us that God is behind everything we eat. God sprinkles snow, releases rain, raises and lowers the sun, tugs on the moon, and crafts creation in a way that sustains life.

When we become more thoughtful about what we eat, we become more connected and grateful.

> We celebrate the gardens and fields and rain and sun, the one who provides all things.
>
> We remember the farmer and worker whose sacrifices make our meal possible.
>
> We look for ways to embrace those across the table and pull up an extra chair.
>
> We begin asking questions about food sources and justice and care for those who provide.

Which of the following would you like to start including in your prayers before meals? Place a check by each one:

- ☐ God who provides rain and sun and seasons.
- ☐ Thanks and blessing on those who farm and harvest.
- ☐ Prayers that God would heal our land.
- ☐ Remembrance of those who don't have friends or family and need others.
- ☐ Those who are working for healthier, more affordable food for all people.
- ☐ Other:

You're Invited to the Table

In the space below, write out a new prayer you'd like to pray before meals.

Eating reminds us that we cannot exist alone; we are created dependent on others.

Eating reminds us that we are not the creators of life; we belong to the one who creates life.

Read the following passage. Circle the verbs or active words, then underline all mentions of food.

> He makes grass grow for the cattle, and plants for people to cultivate—bringing forth food from the earth: wine that gladdens human hearts, oil to make their faces shine, and bread that sustains their hearts. (Psalm 104:14–15)

This passage reveals that food is not a commodity as much as it is a gift of grace. Eating together invites us to become more attentive and taste and see the Lord's goodness with greater spiritual depth. Shared meals can become a place to enter into deeper relationships with one another and God.

Review your daily schedule over the next two weeks. Find time for at least one meal that you can share with someone that's not rushed or hurried. If appropriate, say your new prayer before you eat together.

Taste and See

 CLOSING PRAYER

Spend time asking God to expand your capacity for gratitude before, during, and after meals. Ask God to reveal what he's really giving you as you eat.

DAY FOUR: READ AND LEARN

Read chapter 2 of the *Taste and See* book, "A Flaky Filet of Fish." Use the space below to note any insights or questions you want to share at the next group session.

What surprised you most about Margaret's time fishing on the Sea of Galilee with Ido?

Margaret describes the disciples leaving their full nets to follow Jesus:

> We read this famous fishing story today with the advantage of knowing that those boats and nets will serve a purpose again. But in the moment, the disciples believe they're leaving them forever. They give up their

transportation, their livelihoods, their futures, not to mention the biggest catch of their lives. They've just won the fishing lottery, but they leave it behind for something far better." (p. 41)

Describe a time when Jesus called you to leave something behind for something far better.

Margaret writes:

"If you stop looking to Jesus as your powerhouse, you may start thinking God is overlooking you, ignoring you, or worse yet, punishing you. If you close your eyes too long to God's presence, you may convince yourself that somehow God has rejected you, or worse, has abandoned you altogether. You'll grow deaf to the One who calls from the shore, the One who wants to fill your nets with the impossible and unimaginable." (p. 45)

When are you most tempted to start believing God performs his greatest works in other locations, in other people, in other situations and forget God wants to perform miracles here, now, today?

Where do you need to experience the power of God in your life right now? Write a prayer in the space below.

DAY FIVE: TASTE AND SEE EXPERIENCES

Choose one (or more) of the following activities to grow more intentional in your relationships with one other and God.

1. Go on a picnic. Get outside (or inside, depending on the time of year) with a friend and be intentional about your conversation and time of connection. Consider using the four questions from the video teaching to connect on a deeper relational level.

2. Make one of your favorite recipes or try a new one (you'll find a collection of tasty ones in the *Taste and See* book) and share with your immediate neighbors. As you cook, pray for each family and home. Ask God to open opportunities for deeper connection and kindness.

3. Plant fresh herbs. Consider using seeds or purchasing inexpensive starter plants of spices such as rosemary, basil, thyme, or lemongrass. Then, as they grow, share with neighbors, friends, or even a local food bank.

4. Help others in your community in one of these ways:
   - Purchase food for a local food bank.
   - Volunteer to serve food at a homeless shelter.
   - Scour your pantry shelves and kitchen cabinets for food you can give away (pay attention to expiration dates).
   - Cook for someone who is experiencing long-term health issues, recently gave birth, or is housebound.

Delighting in the Sweetness of Fruitfulness

HOMEWORK GROUP DISCUSSION

Reflecting on all you've read in the *Taste and See* book and the homework you did in the Bible study guide, what stood out to you most?

GETTING STARTED (10–15 minutes)

TASTY ACTIVITY: A FUN FRUIT TASTING

What you'll need:

- Visit a local grocery store's produce section and purchase the most unusual fruit you can find—along with some more common ones. If possible, include dates, pomegranates, and figs. You may want to snap a photo of the fruit's name to help you remember it. Ask the produce manager or research online the best way to eat the fruit.

- Toothpicks

- Plates

1. Cut up the fruit before the gathering and invite everyone to sample the different fruits.

2. Discuss the following:
   - How many of the fruits were new to each person? Which was their favorite? Least favorite?

Delighting in the Sweetness of Fruitfulness 39

- What fruits have you ever grown or tended in your life?
- What do you imagine when you picture a fruitful life with God?

 PLAY SESSION 2 VIDEO (20 minutes)

> See the full recipe for roasted figs and Brussels sprouts in the Recipe Index at the back of this study guide.

NOTES

Adam and Eve commit the first sin by misusing fruit, yet despite this, God continues using fruit and fruit imagery to draw people back to himself.

Dried figs and fig cakes were the energy bars of the ancient world.

"Everyone under their own vine and under their own fig tree." (1 Kings 4:25)

Fig trees are large and leafy.

Fig trees produce multiple harvests.

Fig trees are monochromatic.

Fig trees' fruit ripens slowly.

Through the fig tree, we see God's promise of provision, protection, and presence.

VIDEO DISCUSSION

1. What in today's teaching had the most impact on you?

2. Ask someone to read 1 Samuel 25:18 and 1 Samuel 30:12. What roles do figs play in each of these passages? How is this consistent with Margaret's description of figs in the ancient world?

3. Select three volunteers to read aloud each of the following verses: 1 Kings 4:25; Micah 4:3; and Zechariah 3:10. How does today's teaching impact the way you read these passages?

4. Turn to Luke 19:1–10 and have someone read the passage aloud. The Hebrew name for sycamore-fig is *shikma*, meaning "rehabilitate." In what specific ways was Zacchaeus "rehabilitated" into a whole new life in Christ? In what specific ways have you sensed Christ has rehabilitated you?

5. How does understanding the fig trees and their fruit shift the way you see the fruitfulness in your life right now?

6. In what area of your life are you currently most tempted to fall into striving? What do you need to put on your "to don't" list in order to experience a more satisfying, fruitful life with God?

Delighting in the Sweetness of Fruitfulness 43

7. Which of the following do you need to experience more of in your life right now: God's provision, protection, or presence? Explain.

See Bible Memory Verse p. 125

 **BEFORE THE GROUP ENDS . . .**

Next session's Tasty Activity is called "A Bread Tasting." Review the details of the activity on page 56. Ask for three or more volunteers to commit to bring the food and supplies so the cost and responsibility are shared. If your group chooses to skip the activity, you can still engage in the discussion questions.

 ## CLOSING PRAYER

As you close in prayer, ask:
- God to make his provision, protection, and presence real to every person.
- The Holy Spirit to reveal anything that may be holding anyone back from the fruitful, satisfying life God intends.
- God to expand each participant's capacity to taste and see God's goodness.

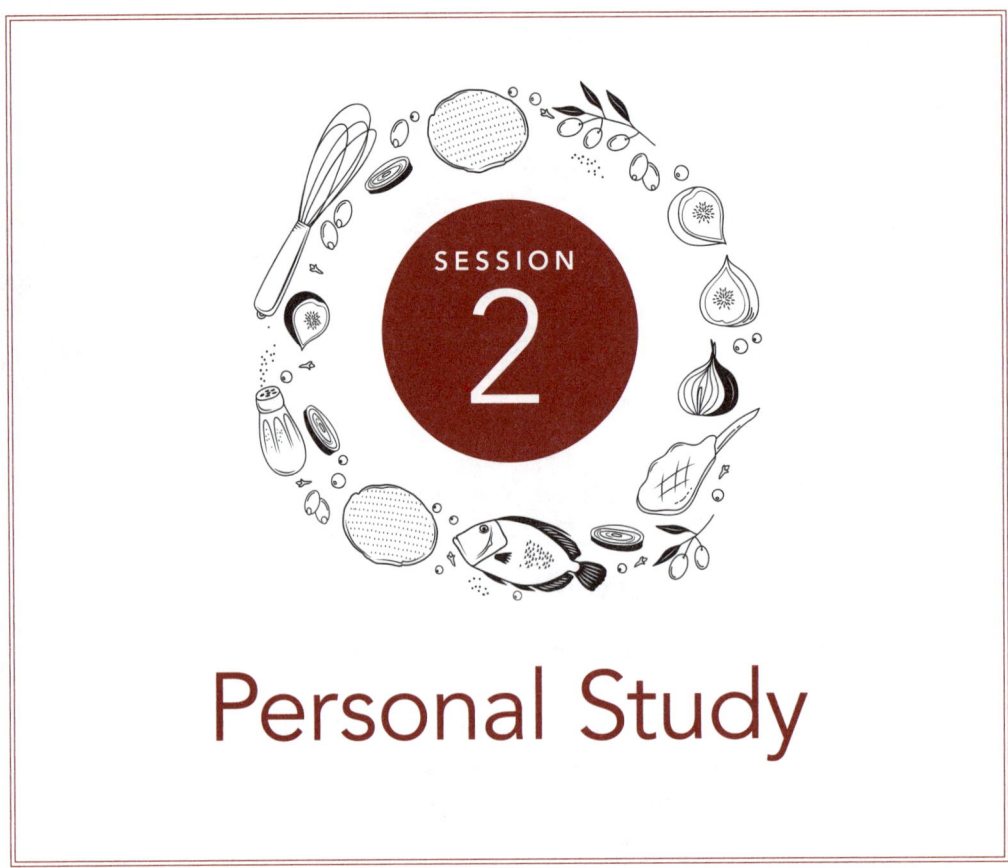

Personal Study

DAY ONE: THE IMPORTANCE OF FRUIT IN THE BIBLE

Fruit trees played a significant role in biblical times, because of their ability to produce much-needed food and provide variety and sweet treats for the people. If a person grew a particular fruit, they could trade it for other fruits or supplies and nourish their families. The Old Testament overflows with frequent mentions of fruit and instructions regarding the care of fruit trees.

Delighting in the Sweetness of Fruitfulness

Read Deuteronomy 20:19. What instruction are the people given regarding trees that produce fruit (versus those that don't; see v. 20)? What is God trying to grow in the people's hearts through this instruction?

Not only does God's instruction protect sustainable food resources, but it also speaks of God's redeeming work in previously occupied lands. Though destruction may take place as an enemy's land is occupied, the people must not live in the land with those same destructive tendencies.

Read Leviticus 19:23. What's the required age of a tree before fruit may be harvested? What must be done on the fourth year?

When I asked Kevin, the fig farmer, about this instruction, he responded, "That follows perfectly with the lifecycle of the fig."

The first year a fig won't produce any fruit, and depending on the variety, you may see a handful the second year. The third year will produce more, but the fourth year is the one that will yield a substantial crop. Thus, God is asking you to give away 100 percent of your biggest crop after all your hard work and waiting.

Interestingly, the grape follows this same harvest cycle.

What is God trying to grow in the people's hearts through this instruction?

What do you sense God trying to grow through you as you give generously and walk in obedience?

QUOTABLE: Likewise, every good tree bears good fruit, but a bad tree bears bad fruit. A good tree cannot bear bad fruit, and a bad tree cannot bear good fruit. Every tree that does not bear good fruit is cut down and thrown into the fire. Thus, by their fruit you will recognize them." –Matthew 7:17–20

Read Galatians 5:22–23. List the fruit of the Spirit below. Place a check mark by each one that would have likely sprouted in the people's hearts as they followed the instructions of Deuteronomy 20:19 and Leviticus 19:23.

☐

☐

☐

☐

☐

☐

☐

☐

☐

On the continuum below, mark the point which describes you best.

|———————————————————————————————————|
I tend to think of my
fruitfulness as something
I must work to attain.

I tend to think of my
fruitfulness as something
cultivated by God.

Sometimes it's tempting to think that we can make ourselves more fruitful, but this is a gift of God, an act of grace. When Jesus says, in John 3:16, "whoever believes in him [will] have eternal life," he's not speaking as much to the quantity of life as to the quality of life, given by God.

CLOSING PRAYER

Spend some time thanking God for the fruitful work he has done in your life and ask him to cultivate more fruitfulness in you.

DAY TWO: READ AND LEARN

Read chapter 3 of the *Taste and See* book, "A Plate of Tart and Tangy Figs." Use the space below to note any insights or questions you want to share during the next group session.

What surprised you most about the unique ways that figs ripen and are harvested?

Margaret writes:

> " Have you ever noticed that when you expect one thing, your attentiveness dulls to everything else? Psychologists call this "change blindness," a term describing our tendency to miss shifts in our immediate visual environment. We assume that if something dramatic changes right before our eyes, we will, of course, recognize the shift. But actually, it's impossible for the human mind to fully process and be aware of every visual detail at all times. " (p. 62)

In what area of your spiritual life are you most prone to change blindness?

What steps do you need to take to live expectant of Christ's work in your life?

Margaret writes:

> **"** Sooner or later we'll all be tempted to believe that our best days are behind us. We'll measure ourselves more by what we can no longer do than by what we still can. We'll feel washed up and washed out. But the fig tree challenges this expectation, too. One of the beauties of the fig tree is that, once planted, it will continue to produce fruit for eighty to a hundred years. **"** (pp. 66–67)

In what areas of your life are you most tempted to believe your best days are behind you? What is Christ's vision for your days ahead?

DAY THREE: THE GIFT OF PRUNING

While visiting the fig farm in the winter, I was surprised by how much the fig trees were pruned back. Yet Kevin explained that hearty pruning is crucial for the fruit's growth.

"Fig pruning is an artform," he said. "And we're very selective about who we allow to prune our trees."

The first time a fig tree is planted, the tree should be cut back by half in order to focus the tree's energy on growing deeper roots and becoming well established. The next pruning will be during the winter season, when the tree is dormant. Toward the bottom of the tree, the pruner must target the suckers on the lower branches and shoots near the roots that rise like periscopes. These must be cut away to ensure the nutrients reach the new growth.

As the tree continues to mature, limbs that do not produce fruit must be pruned. Any dead and diseased wood must also be removed. This helps prevent disease from spreading to other areas of the tree.

Read John 15:2. How does the practice of pruning figs parallel the practice of pruning grapes?

In what areas of your life do you feel like you're currently being pruned by God? Name two or three, if possible.

The scene of a fig branch trimmed here and a shoot snipped there, taking deeper cuts throughout, reminded me of God's gracious hand in pruning. Maybe like me, you've had areas of fruitfulness in your life whacked away, and you wonder, *God, what are you thinking?* Or maybe, like me, you've wondered, *In this area of my life, God, why am I not more fruitful?*

Delighting in the Sweetness of Fruitfulness 51

Yet God remains at work in our innermost being. A snip here, a cut there. We feel the pinch as unproductive shoots are removed. Yet we trust that as the Master Gardener, God is cutting us back so we become more fruitful.

God hand-trims us—holding every branch, nestling his presence into every fiber of our being—with loving patience and tender care. He knows exactly what's needed for a harvest of sweet tangy goodness to blossom and mature in us.

When in your past have you gone through a season of pruning that yielded more fruitfulness?

How does understanding some of the techniques of pruning figs encourage you to submit to God's pruning in your life?

 CLOSING PRAYER

Pause to give God thanks for the pruning he has done in your life. Courageously ask God to prune you more to yield more fruitfulness.

DAY FOUR: READ AND LEARN

As you prepare for next week's session, read chapter 4 of the *Taste and See* book, "A Loaf of Bread Just Out of the Oven." Use the space below to note any insights or questions you want to share during the next group session.

What surprised you most about Margaret's time baking bread with Andrew?

Margaret writes:

> The Israelites have known only enslavement for generations. The honeyed bread of heaven contrasts with the stale bread of their sweaty toil in Egypt. Now God promises to feed his children for free and give them an entire day of rest each week. The offer seems too ridiculous, too foreign, too unbelievable. (p. 84)

How did God use the provision of manna to liberate the hearts of the Israelites from the ways of Egypt?

Margaret describes becoming more attentive to not wasting bread. How can you become more attentive to not wasting food?

Margaret writes:

> With every morsel of manna, God whispers that we are never meant to go it alone. With every morsel of communion, God whispers that we are never meant to go it alone. (p. 88)

How does the communal act of harvesting and making bread in antiquity shift the way you read mentions of bread in the Bible?

How does this communal nature affect the way you take Holy Communion or the Eucharist?

DAY FIVE: TASTE AND SEE EXPERIENCES

Choose one (or more) of the following activities to grow more intentional in your relationships with one another and with God this week.

1. Pick up some unusual fruits from the grocery store as suggested in the group session's opening activity and share them with your family. Talk about the unique flavors and the goodness of God in creating each one.

2. Paint or draw a picture of the fruitful life you want God to give you. Use your creativity to create a beautiful visual prayer to God.

3. Research the term "food deserts" and "food insecurity" to better understand these needs the United States, and consider ways you can help.

4. Make jam, jelly, or dehydrate various fruits and give them away as gifts.

Chewing on the Bread of Life

HOMEWORK GROUP DISCUSSION

Reflecting on all you've read in the *Taste and See* book and the homework you did in the Bible study guide, what stood out to you most?

GETTING STARTED (10–15 minutes)

TASTY ACTIVITY: A BREAD TASTING

What you'll need:
- A variety of fresh loaves of bread including white, wheat, dark, and corn flours. Make sure to include gluten-free options. Try ciabatta, baguettes, and other artisanal varieties.
- Butter, goat's butter, nut butter, cream cheese, or other fun toppings
- Plates
- Knives
- Napkins

1. Invite everyone to sample the different breads.

2. Discuss the following:

    - Which of the breads and toppings were your favorite? Which of the textures and consistencies and flavors of the breads stood out to you most?

    - If Jesus is the Bread of Life, what kind of bread do you think he is? Why?

(**Note:** During research for this session, I asked a variety of bakers this question. Their answers: *French baguette. Kalamata olive bread. Ciabatta. Naan. Challah. Rye. And so many more.* No one said the dime-sized dry communion wafer that melts into a sticky goo and leaves you with questionable breath after a church service. Though each person had experienced a more-than-fair share of life's disappointments, and some remained scabbed and scarred by experiences in the church, the question of bread seemed to slice through the layers of pain. No one listed burnt toast or a charred, rock-hard biscuit. Most people tend to choose a bread they like and often love.)

 PLAY SESSION 3 VIDEO (21 minutes)

> See the full recipe for eighteen-minute matzo in the Recipe Index at the back of this study guide.

NOTES

In the ancient world, the diet consisted of bread, bread, and more bread.

The most common flours in the ancient world were always darker in color, because these grains proved easier to grow, more resilient to drought, and produced a higher yield.

In the Scripture, bread offers more than a metaphor for sustaining life; bread literally keeps people alive.

The Bread of Life came to change the way we live life.

By combining "watch out" and "beware," Jesus creates a double exclamation point regarding the leaven of the Pharisees and Sadducees.

Jesus knew the same leaven that created the teachings of the Pharisees and Sadducees can rise in our hearts, too.

All too often it's easier to recognize *someone else's* legalism, judgmentalism, religiosity, power-hungry nature—and remain blind to our own.

The antidote to the leaven of sin is Christ's work in us.

VIDEO DISCUSSION

1. When you think of bread, what problems, issues, or struggles come to mind?

2. How do you think these struggles affect the way you think about Jesus as the Bread of Life?

3. Have you previously noticed the significant role that bread plays in the Bible? Which mention from Margaret's teaching stood out to you most and why?

4. Open your Bibles to Matthew 16:6–12 and have a volunteer read the passage aloud. What is Jesus' response to leaven?

5. How can leaven affect not just an individual but an entire group of people?

6. Margaret says, "The judgmental nature, the critical eye, the insidious pride we notice in others, wait to rise up in us, too." In what area of your life do you find this happening to you?

Chewing on the Bread of Life 61

7. How does the Bread of Life want to change the way you live? The way you treat others?

See Bible Memory Verse p. 125

BEFORE THE GROUP ENDS . . .

Next session's Tasty Activity is called "A Salt Tasting." Review the details of the activity on pages 76–77. Ask for three or more volunteers to commit to bring the food and supplies so the cost and responsibility are shared. If your group chooses to skip the activity, you can still engage in the discussion questions.

 CLOSING PRAYER

As you close in prayer, ask:
- God to expand each participant's capacity to taste and see God's goodness.
- The Holy Spirit to reveal any areas where leaven's judgmentalism or cynicism try to arise this week.
- That each participant would experience the Bread of Life changing the way life is lived.

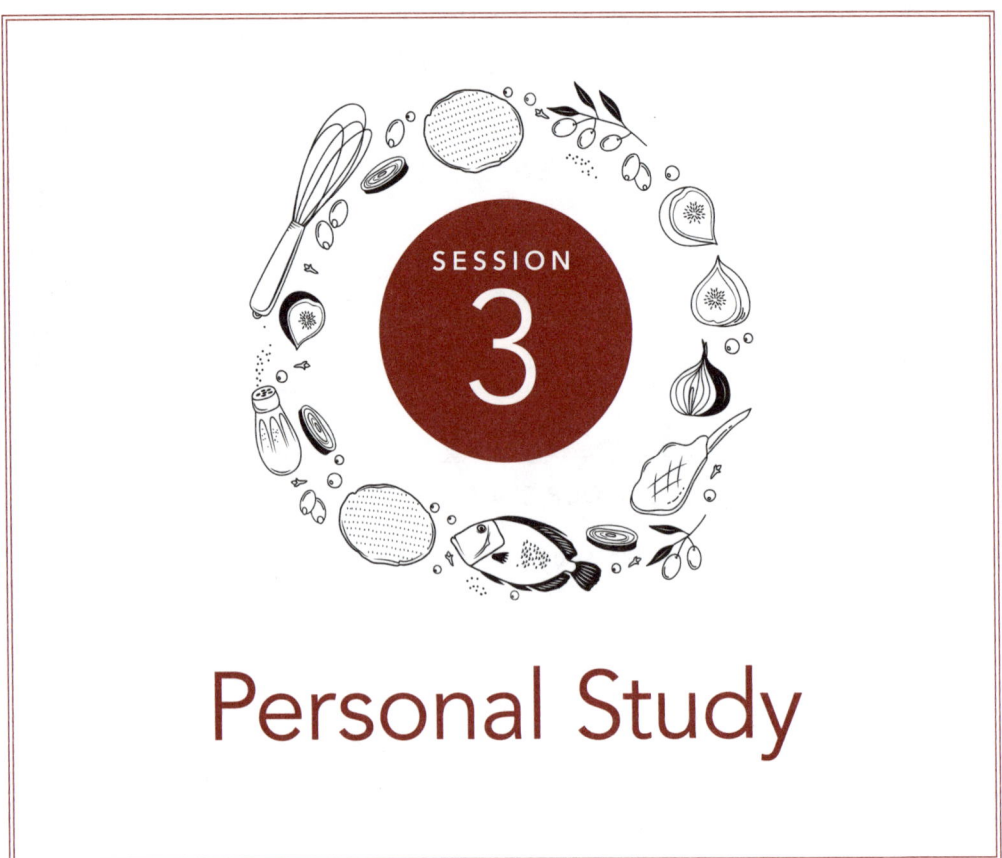

Personal Study

DAY ONE: TOGETHERNESS IN BREAD

When I asked William Rubel, one of the world's foremost bread historians, which bread he loves most, he described two different loaves. A rye bread he ate in Lithuania during the Soviet period that was thick with cement grit since the flour was ground on a poorly graded grindstone. The second loaf was part of a Coptic Easter celebration in Ethiopia. A woman had ground the flour by hand for eight hours before baking the loaf in a Dutch oven over a wood fire.

What intrigued me about Rubel's responses is that he didn't just remember a piece of a loaf in isolation. The bread was connected to the people, to the place, to the cooking environment. But this isn't true just for him. Bread is embedded in a social interaction, a particular place, and surrounded by rich memories.

"The best bread experiences are shared," Rubel said.

What's the most favorite bread you've ever eaten? Describe the surrounding situation.

Sketch an image of that moment in the space below.

Now envision Jesus instructing his followers to take and eat in remembrance of him during the Last Supper. Imagine the scent of the bread, the crunch of the crumb, the conversation around the table, the miraculous provision of a place to celebrate the Passover.

The bread that was broken was never eaten or experienced in a vacuum but embedded in the memories of the disciples by the surrounding taste and sight and touch and sound. Scientists have discovered a direct link between the brain region responsible for taste memory and the area responsible for remembering the time and place we experienced the food.[3]

Read Matthew 26:26–30. What do you think the disciples experienced in each of the following areas?

SIGHTS:

SOUNDS:

SMELLS:

TEXTURES:

Chewing on the Bread of Life 65

TASTES:

> **NOTABLE:** Bread is intimately linked to the companionship around the table as the loaf is passed, cut, torn, chewed. The word "companion" is derived from the Latin *com* meaning "with" and *panis* meaning "bread."

When we receive the bread as part of Holy Communion, we are given an opportunity to taste home and hospitality, to taste companionship and compassion, fellowship and friendship, affection and affirmation. Bread is more than sharing a morsel or meal together; it's sharing life together.

Who are three people you want to be intentional about sharing bread and life with over the next six weeks? Write their names below:

-
-
-

What steps can you take to be intentional about developing these relationships and sharing table time together?

CLOSING PRAYER

Take some time to ask God to bring to mind people who he is nudging you to spend time with. As names or faces come to mind, reach out to each one.

DAY TWO: OUR DAILY BREAD

Throughout Jesus' life and ministry, he retreats up mountainsides to pray. In the Sermon on the Mount, Jesus offers specific instruction on how to pray as well as how *not* to pray.

Read Matthew 6:5. How does Jesus tell us *not* to pray? In what ways are you tempted to pray like this?

Read Matthew 6:6–8. How does Jesus instruct us *to* pray? In what ways are you committed to praying like this?

Jesus goes on to give the famous words that have become the Lord's Prayer. Read Matthew 6:9–13. Where is the line "Give us today our daily bread" located within the prayer?

The central location of this request within the prayer is important considering bread was such a staple for those in the Middle East. For many centuries, scholars have debated the meaning of the Greek word *epiousios*, which can be translated "daily." Does it refer to *time* or the *amount* of bread? Is it one day's worth of bread? The minimal amount of bread to survive?

Scholar Kenneth Bailey notes that a better translation would be:

> "Give us today the bread that doesn't run out."

This translation helps us catch a better glimpse of Jesus' heart behind the prayer. Remember, Jesus is the Bread of Life, and in this prayer he is speaking both to our physical and spiritual needs.

At its heart, this prayer calls us to trust in God that there will be enough. Just as God provided manna in the desert, God will provide for us. This prayer is a heart cry for God to deliver us from the fear of lack.

In what area of your life do you most need deliverance from the fear of not enough?

Living with an unhealthy fear can hold us back from the life God has for us.

Consider some of the effects of living with unhealthy fear. Place a check mark by the ones that you've found true in your life.

Fear causes me to:

- ☐ Lose joy
- ☐ Think irrationally
- ☐ Become more self-focused
- ☐ Cling to safety as a god
- ☐ Become risk-adverse
- ☐ Love less
- ☐ Rely more on myself
- ☐ Forget the goodness of God
- ☐ Other:

Notice that Jesus doesn't ask us to pray, "Give *me* today the bread that doesn't run out," but rather, "Give *us* today the bread that doesn't run out." From the start of the prayer, Jesus focuses on the "us" and "our" instead of the "me" and "mine."

Where in your prayer life do you need to shift your focus from the "me" and "mine" to the "us" and "our"?

Finally, it's worth noting that all bread—or food—ultimately comes from God. He is the One who we trust for today, tomorrow, and forever.

 CLOSING PRAYER

Take a moment to ask God for the Bread that doesn't run out in your life. Ask God to reveal any areas where a fear of lack is holding you back from fully trusting him.

DAY THREE: FINE FLOURS

Five types of sacrifices are commanded in Levitical law—burnt, grain, peace, sin, and trespass offerings. The grain or cereal offering is given after the burnt offering (meat), which represented atonement for sins. The grain that follows is a gift of worship and the most holy of offerings presented to God (Leviticus 2:10). Often this grain offering is made of finely ground flour—a labor of love and generosity. This same flour is also mentioned when serving guests.

Read Genesis 18:6. How much fine flour did Sarah use to prepare bread for the visitors?

Read 1 Kings 4:22. How much fine flour was required daily for Solomon's palace?

Read Leviticus 2:1. What are the ingredients of the grain offering?

Why was fine flour given to Abraham's guests, used in the royal palace, and required for the offering? Much of the answer rests in the process of making this prized food. Fine meal and white flour require more time, energy, and preparation.

QUOTABLE: "Historically, household breads (as opposed to rolls and fine breads for high-status dinners) were baked once a fortnight, and sometimes much less frequently. Among the peasantry it was standard for bread to be consumed at various stages of staling. There were different uses for breads at different points in the staling process. Breads could so stale that pieces cut or hacked out of loaves had to be soaked in water before they could be consumed. Social elites could afford to have bread baked often, or could afford to buy fresh bread from the baker."
–William Rubel in *Bread: A Global History*

To make fine (white) flour, all of the bran and germ must be sifted out. This makes the flour truly white. If you sift 100 pounds of flour, only 10–20 percent will be fine and white. The other 80–90 percent will create coarser, heavier bread. Thus, fine flour was the most prized and sought-after in antiquity.

Sometimes when asking people to give, a church leader will alliterate and ask people to give their time, talent, and treasure. Yet in sacrificing fine flour, all three were involved. A person had to give of their time, talent, and treasure in planting and nurturing the wheat, harvesting the bounty, then sifting through the wheat to offer the best, most desirable, portion.

On the continuum below, mark which describes you best.

•──•
When it comes to giving, I tend to think quantity over quality. When it comes to giving, I tend to think quality over quantity.

In the chart below, list the different ways you're giving and sacrificing right now.

Time	Talent	Treasure

In which area do you tend to be most generous at giving? In which do you tend to be least generous?

What is one thing you could sacrifice or give this week that involves all three?

CLOSING PRAYER

Spend some time asking God how you can give your best to him in a new or fresh way. Ask God to challenge the way you're thinking about giving so that you'll become even more generous.

DAY FOUR: READ AND LEARN

Read chapter 5 of the *Taste and See* book, "A Dash of Sea Salt." Use the space below to note any insights or questions you want to share at the next group session.

What surprised you most about the in-depth history of salt?

Margaret describes the salty judgment of God on Sodom and Gomorrah. Read Ezekiel 16:48–50. What are the sins of Sodom according to this passage? Which of these do you most struggle with in your life right now?

Margaret writes:

> " Sometimes the places Christ sends you will feel manure-like—the last places, the last people, the last situations you'd ever want to engage. Like Jonah, you may be tempted to resist the hardship, the discomfort, the awkwardness and stinkiness, and stay in your comfort zone. Yet, it's your salty fertilizer that brings salvation to a dysfunctional and dying world. " (p. 115)

Where is the stinkiest place Christ is calling you to right now? What's stopping you from obeying?

Who is the person in your life that you sense God calling you to ease of their pain?

DAY FIVE: TASTE AND SEE EXPERIENCES

Choose one (or more) of the following activities to grow more intentional in your relationships with one another and God.

1. Consider gathering a group from your church to offer to bake bread for an upcoming communion service (remembering our gluten-free friends too). If possible, add a little honey to remind your taste buds of manna.

2. Review your notes from the video and homework sessions and reflect on 1 Corinthians 11:23–24. Reflect on how your fresh understanding of bread enhances your understanding of Holy Communion.

3. Prepare a loaf of bread as an act of prayer and worship. Consider the steps involved. As you mix the ingredients, ask God to reveal the deeper work he is doing in you. As you knead, ask God to show how he is pushing and pulling you into a closer relationship with him. As you wait for the bread to rise, ask God to reveal the transformative work he's doing in your life. As you enjoy the bread, ask God how you can taste and see his goodness more in your life.

4. Invite a friend to make eighteen-minute matzo with you. Use the recipe from the back of this study guide. Ask God to open opportunities for deeper connection as you bake together.

SESSION 4

Savoring the Salt of the Earth

 Taste and See

📖 HOMEWORK GROUP DISCUSSION

Reflecting on all you've read in the *Taste and See* book and the homework you did in the Bible study guide, what stood out to you most?

GETTING STARTED (10–15 minutes)

TASTY ACTIVITY: A SALT TASTING

What you'll need:
- 4–6 different types of salt that vary in color, texture, and region: such as kosher, Himalayan, smoked, grey sea salt, salt-free salt, and others
- A selection of salt-friendly foods such as plain bread or crackers (don't forget a gluten-free option), cucumbers, chocolate, tomatoes, mozzarella, watermelon, or a combination of any of these
- Non-salted butter (if bread is used)
- Small plates
- Napkins

1. Invite the participants to try the salts (as their health adviser allows) and notice which part of the tongue is most sensitive to salt flavors and how salt changes as you taste it.

2. As participants taste each salt, invite them to write down some of the descriptive notes in their study guide, including their preferences as well

Savoring the Salt of the Earth

as the size, shape, and color of the crystals. Take note of the various flavors such as mild, strong, abrasive, smoky, floral, and sweet.

3. Discuss the following:

- Which salt was your favorite and why?

- Which salt was your least favorite and why?

- What does it mean to you when Jesus says, "You are the salt of the earth"?

 PLAY SESSION 4 VIDEO (21 minutes)

> See the full recipe for dark chocolate sea salt cookies (gluten-free) in the Recipe Index at the back of this study guide.

NOTES

Sal in Latin means salt. That's where we get the word "salary." Or the expressions "earning his salt" and "worth her salt."

Just as salt is placed between the layers in curing fish and meat, so too you are embedded in this culture, in this place, in this time, in this slice of history.

Jesus is saying, as the salt of the earth, everywhere you go, you're going to bring the taste of heaven down to earth.

When salt is overpowered by the presence of other things, it loses its ability to influence.

When Jesus warns us about losing our saltiness, he's not talking about table salt; he's talking about fertilizer salt.

The word for "salvation" shares the same Latin root as "salt."

You are an agent of preservation, flavoring, and human flourishing.

VIDEO DISCUSSION

1. Open your Bibles to Matthew 5:1–12. Select three volunteers to read aloud four verses each. How does Jesus' opening to the Sermon on the Mount set up the declaration, "You are the salt of the earth"? What in Jesus' words equip us to be salt?

2. Read Matthew 5:13 aloud. How is Christ asking you to be a preserving agent, one who preserves the ways, the teachings, the presence of Christ, right where you are in your life?

3. Where are you being challenged to be a flavoring agent—bringing people forgiveness where there's bitterness or introducing the sweetness of Christ where there's sourness?

4. What are some practical ways you can bring the flavor of heaven down here to earth?

5. Margaret says, "When salt is overpowered by the presence of other things, it loses its ability to influence." How are you being tempted to lose your saltiness right now?

6. Leader, read Luke 14:35 aloud to the group. How did your understanding of "salt of the earth" change when you learned that Jesus is describing fertilizing salt?

7. In what ways have you been feeling overwhelmed by the many needs all around you? How does identifying one person or situation you can help flourish make that less overwhelming?

See Bible Memory Verse p. 125

Savoring the Salt of the Earth 81

>
>
> **BEFORE THE GROUP ENDS . . .**
>
> Next session's Tasty Activity is called "An Olive and Olive Oil Tasting." Review the details of the activity on pages 98–99. Ask for three or more volunteers to commit to bring the food and supplies so the cost and responsibility are shared. If your group chooses to skip the activity, you can still engage in the discussion questions.

CLOSING PRAYER

As you close in prayer, ask:
- God to expand each participant's capacity to taste and see God's goodness.
- The Holy Spirit to reveal where God is calling each person to be salt.
- That each participant would have opportunities to be an agent of preserving, flavoring, and human flourishing.

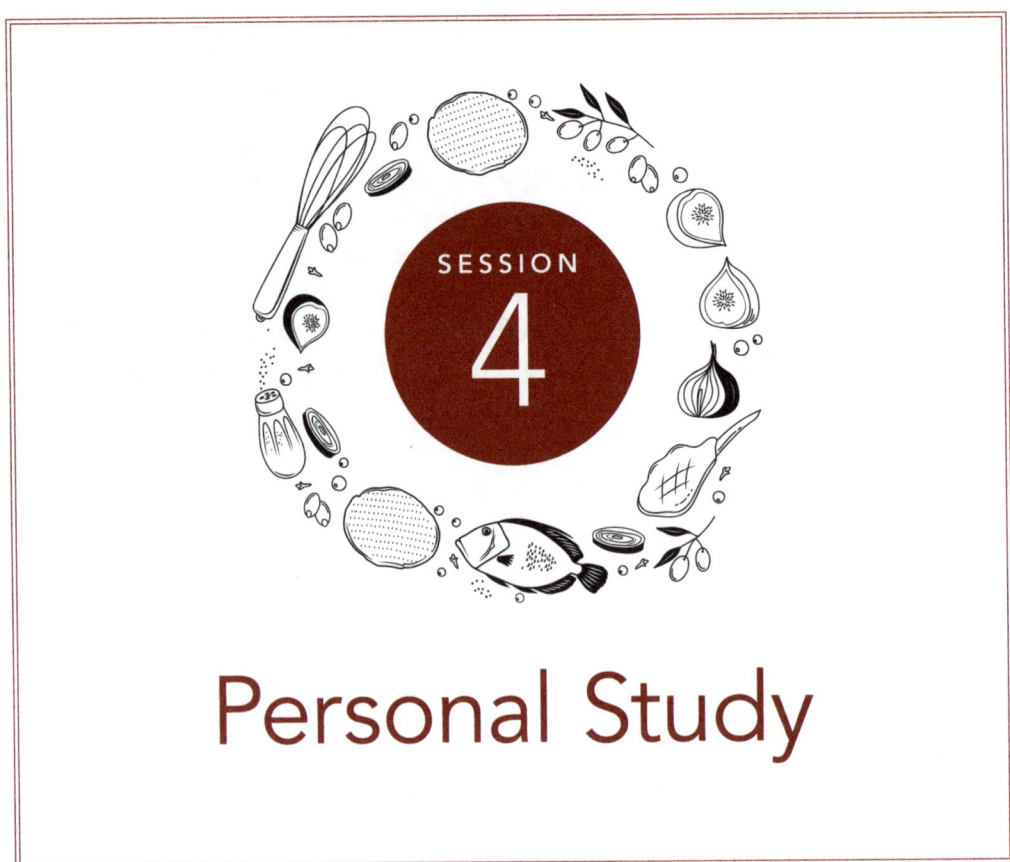

Personal Study

DAY ONE: SALT COVENANTS

God provides the most delectable way to connect with humanity: salt. Our bodies depend on it; our taste buds dance to it; God uses it to teach us about his promises. Who can forget a fellow salt aficionado, Job, who asks, "Can that which is tasteless be eaten without salt?"[4]

One the most notable mentions of salt in the Bible is in association with salt covenants. In the Old Testament, such a reference is made three times.

In each of the following passages, what are the instructions given regarding salt? Who are they given to?

	Instruction	Recipient
Leviticus 2:13		
Numbers 18:19		
2 Chronicles 13:5		

God initiates a salt covenant when he asks the Israelites to add the substance, first to their grain offerings, then to all their offerings. God then uses salt covenants to remind the priests of his ongoing care, and the kings of his promises. The term, salt covenant, plays off of the nature of salt. Sodium chloride, also known as table salt, was the ancient world's natural refrigerator, a mineral preservative which prevented bacteria from growing. By adding salt, food was kept from rotting, remaining unchanged, effectively permanent.

The Hebrew word for covenant, *běriyth*, means an agreement between two parties, based in trust, to each fulfill their end of the deal. Why did God initiate the salt covenants? To reveal his indissoluble relationship with his people. In each instance, God is asking the people, priests, and kings to enter into a permanent commitment to his purposes.

QUOTABLE: "On Friday nights Jews dip the Sabbath bread in salt. In Judaism, bread is a symbol of food, which is a gift from God, and dipping the bread in salt preserves it—keeps the agreement between God and his people." –Mark Kurlansky in *Salt: A World History*

In the ancient world, after creating a covenant, both parties shared salt to show the binding, permanent nature of the promise. If one side broke their obligations, the offended party threw excessive amounts of salt onto the others' land, making the ground infertile and useless for agriculture.

Of course, the Lord never breaks a promise. His plans will not be thwarted and his promise to his people, even though they often fail, is unchanging, permanent, and everlasting.

Read Numbers 23:19. What does this verse reveal about God's promises?

As Joshua, who led the Israelites after Moses, was nearing death, he said, "And now I am about to go the way of all the earth, and you know in your hearts and souls, all of you, that not one word has failed of all the good things that the Lord your God promised concerning you. All have come to pass for you; not one of them has failed" (Joshua 23:14 ESV).

How have you found this to be true in your life?

Read the following three promises. Circle the one you most need to hear right now. Why is the promise particularly meaningful at this time?

Savoring the Salt of the Earth

- "The LORD will fight for you; you need only to be still." (Exodus 14:14)
- "He gives strength to the weary and increases the power of the weak." (Isaiah 40:29)
- "If any of you lacks wisdom, you should ask God, who gives generously to all without finding fault, and it will be given to you." (James 1:5)

CLOSING PRAYER

Ask God to reveal one Bible verse to you in this upcoming week that you can cling to in this season of your life.

DAY TWO: SPICES OF THE BIBLE

One of my favorite additions to any recipe is fresh spices. Something about the fragrance and flavors makes food dance with deliciousness. While we connect spices to cooking, those living in antiquity often connected spices to nonculinary uses.

Herbs first sprout in Eden but pop up throughout Scripture, from the bitter herbs used to commemorate the Passover to King Solomon's garden. Thistle and thyme, myrrh and mint, cumin and coriander, these biblical herbs were—and, in some cases, still are—used in medicine, cosmetics, perfumes, ritual practices, and embalming.

Read Song of Songs 4:14. Note each of the spices listed in this passage.

-
-
-
-
-
-
-

Not all of the spices mentioned in the Bible clearly translate to what we know and understand today. Yet some are still understood and used today.

QUOTABLE: "The herbs and spices considered indispensable in the modern kitchen make our food taste better, more exotic, and, with the advent of greater nutritional awareness, we know that they have the potential to make us healthier. Our biblical ancestors, however, did not always connect herbs and spices to food; sometimes they were entirely unrelated to it. Non-food uses for spices were extensive." —Miriam Feinberg Vamosh in *Food at the Time of the Bible*

Nard, also known as spikenard, was used for perfume and also used as a sedative.

Saffron comes from a flower whose pistils are dried and used in dye, cooking, and perfume.

Cinnamon comes from the bark of a cinnamon tree that was native to China before being introduced to the Holy Land. It was one of the ingredients in the incense which was used in the tabernacle (Exodus 30:22–32).

Myrrh is famed for being a gift from the Magi to the Christ child (Matthew 2:11), but the fragrance is mentioned throughout the Bible (Genesis 37:25; Exodus 30:23; Psalm 45:8). It was also used to make less desirable wine more drinkable. This is why it's mentioned in the wine offered to Jesus on the cross (Mark 15:23).

Aloes in the Bible are thought to come from the eaglewood tree imported from India. This is different than the aloes or agave enjoyed in America. These aloes had a strong fragrance that lasted for an extended period of time, making them useful for anointing the dead—including the body of Jesus (John 19:39).[5]

What are your favorite herbs? Your favorite uses for them?

Biblical law required a tithe—giving a tenth of what one had to the temple—and this included agricultural produce. The religious leaders naturally wondered how far the command extended. If they tithed from their sheep and wheat, should they go as far as to tithe from their spices too?

The Pharisees were torn over this issue. Some argued that spices needed to be tithed; others believe that was not required by the law. This is the debate that Jesus enters into when he finds himself invited into the home of a Pharisee. The host is surprised when Jesus doesn't engage in ritual handwashing. Jesus calls them to be generous with the poor and everything will be clean with them. Then Jesus challenges their thinking on tithing spices.

Read Luke 11:42. What do you think Jesus is communicating in this statement?

Jesus sides with no one. Instead, he calls out each of their blind spots. The Pharisees use magnifying glasses on the most minuscule details of the law but miss the big picture: justice, faith, and mercy.

Jesus uses a hyperbole when he calls out mint, dill, and cumin. The point of the law was never about herbs. Yet the Pharisees bicker over the tiniest of seasonings, when their hearts are calloused toward others. God requires mercy, not sacrifice.

Describe a time you found yourself so focused on right-versus-wrong that you missed an opportunity to love someone.

Jesus' rebukes center on the Pharisees' pride. They know the law inside and out, backward and forward, but miss its intent. They think they understand, but instead their knowledge is their biggest obstacle. Their religion is laden with legalism.

Savoring the Salt of the Earth

Who are three people that you've missed the opportunity to love because you were focused on minor details rather than the big picture of God's story?

-
-
-

Perhaps they vote differently than you, parent differently, dress differently, work a different collared job, exist in a different tax bracket, or attend a different church.

How can you show mercy and love to them instead of judgment and condemnation?

 CLOSING PRAYER

Spend time asking God to reveal any areas in your life where you've become more focused on becoming right rather than righteous. Ask God to help you to become humbler and more compassionate.

DAY THREE: FAITH LIKE A MUSTARD SEED

Somedays, my faith can seem downright dinky. Doubt slithers in. Prayer moves to the back burner. I second guess. I take things into my own hands. I wonder if God is even listening—if God is too busy for me.

I take comfort that Jesus refers to a downright dinky seed when he speaks about faith.

If you visit the Holy Land, you may notice the mustard plant which grows rapidly in fields and along roads. In the spring, you can pick out these plants by their white or yellow blossoms. One of the unique features of the mustard plant is the speed at which it grows. This is an invasive species that grows fast and large. Given the right amount of sunlight, a little water, rich soil, and the tender care of a Good Farmer, mustard seeds sprout into shrubs that scale three to nine feet in the air.

Read Matthew 17:14–21. What is the setting for Jesus' comments about the mustard seed?

The divine irony behind the mustard seed is that what you see isn't what you get. Mustard seeds are only one to two millimeters in diameter, but what they lack in girth, they make up for in hardiness.

Jesus' mention of the mustard seed highlights the humble beginnings of a tiny seed as well as the colossal potential hidden inside.

Savoring the Salt of the Earth

Read Luke 17:5–6. In the space below draw a branch with 6–10 oversized mustard seeds. Inside each one, name an area of your life where you would most like to grow in faith.

Jesus' multiple mentions of mustard seeds suggests how common this spice was in the lives of people he teaches. Living in an agricultural context means they are familiar with the growth and development of this plant. Jesus compares the kingdom of heaven to a mustard seed.

Read Matthew 13:31–32. In what ways is the kingdom of heaven like a mustard seed?

Jesus' example is less about how much or little faith rests in you and more about the largeness of the God in whom your faith rests.

What encouragement do you find in knowing that you are part of something that's bigger than yourself?

CLOSING PRAYER

Spend time asking God to reveal any stumbling blocks to your faith. Ask God for the ability to trust more, no matter what the situation or circumstance.

DAY FOUR: READ AND LEARN

Read chapter 6 of the *Taste and See* book, "A Delectable Bowl of Olives." Use the space below to note any insights or questions you want to share at the next group session.

What surprised you most about the adventures in Olivedom?

Margaret describes the story of the widow and multiplied oil in 2 Kings 4:1–7. As you read this passage, what are the different miracles you see? What miracle do you most need in your life right now?

Margaret writes:

> "We are called to be people who give and receive anointing and prayer. The act itself can be healing as we make ourselves vulnerable, allow someone to enter our space and physically touch us, to remind us that we are not alone." (p. 141)

What holds you back from asking others to pray for you? What holds you back from praying for others more often?

What's the area in your life that most needs healing? Take a dab of oil and some time to ask God to unleash his healing presence.

Savoring the Salt of the Earth

DAY FIVE: TASTE AND SEE EXPERIENCES

Choose one (or more) of the following activities to grow more intentional in your relationships with one another and God.

1. Read Matthew 26:20–25 and google a high-resolution image of Leonardo DaVinci's painting, *The Last Supper*. Take note in the painting of the location and position of the salt. Since spilling salt was known as a sign that something evil or calamitous was about to happen, what do you think DaVinci was trying to communicate by adding this salty detail to the painting?

2. Create your own smoked salt, place it in small bottles, and give them away as gifts. You'll find a recipe for smoked salt in the *Taste and See* book on page 119.

3. Replace your salt shaker with small dishes filled with specialty salts from your local grocery store. Look for salts from around the world. Invite family members and guests to salt their food with a pinch in the quantity and flavor they prefer. Consider sharing what you've been learning about salt and the Bible with them.

4. Try the gluten-free salted dark chocolate cookie recipe from the video. In one half the batch, try Leif's additions of walnuts and peanut butter chips. In the second half of the batch, leave it plain like Margaret suggests. After you try them both, email Margaret and Leif at hello@margaretfeinberg.com to let us know your favorite.

Relishing the Olive and Its Oil

HOMEWORK GROUP DISCUSSION

Reflecting on all you've read in the *Taste and See* book and the homework you did in the Bible study guide, what stood out to you most?

GETTING STARTED (10–15 minutes)

 ### TASTY ACTIVITY: AN OLIVE AND OLIVE OIL TASTING

What you'll need:
- 4 different types of olives of various colors and textures
- 4 different types of olive oil from various regions
- Bread cut in small tasting squares
- Gluten-free crackers
- Toothpicks
- Small plates
- Napkins

1. Invite the participants to try the olives and olive oil, recognizing that some may prefer to skip the olives and just enjoy the oil sampling.

2. As participants taste the olive and oil samples, invite them to write down some descriptive notes in their study guide, including their preferences. Take note of the various flavors such as aggressive, assertive, or pungent; bitter, delicate, or gentle; rustic, spicy, or sweet.

Relishing the Olive and Its Oil 99

3. Discuss the following:

- Which olive and olive oil were your favorite, and why?

- Which olive and olive oil were your least favorite, and why?

- What do olives and olive oil symbolize to you?

 PLAY SESSION 5 VIDEO (21 minutes)

> See the full recipe for fresh Italian olive oil dip in the Recipe Index at the back of this study guide.

NOTES

The olive leaf is a stunning micro-miracle of creation.

Sometimes God will lead us into places of great discomfort as we walk in obedience and faithfulness to him.

In our worst storms, in the toughest times in life, God will answer us with a double portion of his peace.

Christ, the Messiah, whose name means Anointed One, retreats to the Mount of Olives, located in the Garden of Gethsemane, meaning garden of the olive press.

The olive reminds us that in that which looks dead, there remains life.

The Prince of Peace waits to scoop you up with layers of peace on peace on peace.

Wherever you find yourself, God's peace is already planted there.

VIDEO DISCUSSION

1. What surprised you most about Margaret's stories of harvesting olives? How do her insights shift the way you read passages of Scripture?

2. Open your Bibles to Genesis 8:8–11 and have a volunteer read the passage aloud to the group. In what area of your life have you been sending out a dove as you wait on God?

3. What do you most urgently want to hear from God right now?

4. How will you respond if, like Noah, the answer doesn't come in the way or time you expect?

5. Invite a participant to read Luke 22:39–46 aloud to the group. In what tangible ways had God planted peace for Christ in this scene? (Hint: verse 43)

6. Margaret says, "Wherever you find yourself, God's peace is already planted there." How have you found this to be true in your life?

7. Where do you most need a double portion of God's peace right now?

See Bible Memory Verse p. 125

BEFORE THE GROUP ENDS . . .

Next session's Tasty Activity is called "A Celebration of the Goodness of God." Review the details of the activity on pages 116–117. Ask three participants to bring eating utensils and some simple decorations. Ask for everyone else to commit to bring a food for the celebration party.

CLOSING PRAYER

As you close in prayer, ask:
- God to give everyone a double portion of his peace.
- The Holy Spirit to unleash his anointing presence on each person.
- That each participant would taste and see God's goodness.

Session 5: Personal Study

DAY ONE: THE HEALING YOUR HEART CRAVES

I recently attended a fundraiser for a popular youth organization held in a high school gym. Our assigned table lacked enough chairs. Feelings of rejection flooded my heart as if I were still fifteen.

Leif wrapped his arm around me. We found extra seating and stayed. During the presentation, a video of youth activities flashed across the screen. My body shook. My face flooded with tears. I ran to the restroom to hide. I'd been bullied so much during those years. I choked back the anguish in the bathroom stall. Pain never wears a clock. The agony from decades past sometimes returns without warning, and God stands ready to take flight with healing in his wings.

God had seen a wound, a welt, an open sore . . . and in his physician's love, brought it to the surface for healing.

I slipped back into the gathering and spent the remainder of the time praying for those who had spoken such harshness as well as those who had failed to protect me. Sometimes blessing those who hurt us unleashes the oil of healing. That night when we arrived home, I asked Leif to pray over me and to anoint me with oil, as a symbol of the healing work of the Spirit in me.

Read James 5:14. When was the last time you were anointed with oil and someone prayed for you?

What prevents you from asking for prayer for healing from others more often?

What prevents you from praying for others' healing more often?

All of us have areas where we need healing. Perhaps the healing you need is emotional. The wounds trace back to your youth. You were wounded by disappointments or regret or the realization that life hasn't turned out like you hoped. Your best friend wounded you or you've buried a loved one or you weep over a prodigal who refuses to return home. You'd give anything for things to be different, but even if they were, you know the woundedness would remain.

Maybe you need healing in your body. Maybe you live in chronic pain. Perhaps you face medical challenges or sickness that have left your body reeling. You have visited a hundred doctors, and none have answers. Or maybe you thought you had the cure and it slipped through your fingers.

Perhaps you need healing in your soul. You've held onto bitterness and cynicism for so long that you can't pry yourself free. Many of the wounds and sore afflictions you feel come from your insistence to rebel and run the other way from God.

Or maybe you need healing in your mind to think clearly, to have your wits about you again. To break free of the flashbacks and shaking and trauma that dull your senses. Maybe the chemical imbalances or hormone changes have gnawed away at you. You'd give all you own for healing.

If you're like me, you long for healing that, some days, seems impossible. You live in the chronic pain. You survive on sleeping pills. You're hurting because you're not healed. You, too, need the healing that only God can give.

The call to be anointed with oil is rooted deep in Scripture as an act of compassion, an expression of love, an invitation to healing and wholeness.

Relishing the Olive and Its Oil 107

In the space below, draw a picture of your body, and then identify three areas in your life where you most need healing right now.

 CLOSING PRAYER

Ask God for opportunities to give and receive prayer during the next week—at church, your small group or Bible study, your family, or wherever God may lead.

DAY TWO: READ AND LEARN

Read chapter 7 of the *Taste and See* book, "A Flame-Grilled Lamb Chop." Use the space below to note any insights or questions you want to share at the next group session.

What surprised you most about Margaret's time with the Meat Apostle?

In light of Margaret's insights about livestock in the ancient world, how do you now read Psalm 50:10 differently?

Margaret writes:

> By becoming flesh and offering himself as a sacrifice for humanity, God crossed the great divide from feeling sorry for our pain to being present in our pain. He became, truly, God *with* us. (p. 162)

What does it mean to you to recognize that God doesn't just sympathize with your pain but empathizes with it?

What's the area in your life that most needs rescue? Take some time to ask God to provide rescue for you.

DAY THREE: GOD'S RESILIENCE IN YOU

As Natalija and I walked up the mountainside among the endless maze of olive trees, I was taken aback by how much some of them had been neglected. Some were nothing more than dried rotting stumps. The kind of things you'd look at and think no life could ever come from such dead wood.

Yet Natalija explained that's part of the miracle of the olive. The base of the tree is a root ball which sprouts shoots for centuries. If the tree is consumed by insects, burned by fire, neglected by time, you can still saw away the deadwood and another will grow in its place.

Though the trunks become craggy, bent, and hollow inside, deep in the core, life remains. The roots will sprout fresh tendrils. At the first scent of water it will spring to life again.

The scene reminds me of the truth Job discovered in his darkest hour. Consider Job 14:7–9:

> At least there is hope for a tree: If it is cut down, it will sprout again, and its new shoots will not fail. Its roots may grow old in the ground and its stump die in the soil, yet at the scent of water it will bud and put forth shoots like a plant.

Based on what you know of Job's story, in what ways is his description of an olive tree true in his own life?

In essence, Job, whose life has been reduced to a stump says dead trees can live again.

In what area of your life do you most long for God to sprout new shoots?

The principle of Christ bringing life out of that which appears dead gives us a hope for the future. Even when circumstances and situations and bodies appear wasting away, Christ renews that sprig of life inside us.

Sometimes it's easier to believe in this newness of Christ's work in our lives than in the lives of others. I'm embarrassed to admit how many times I've passed by situations and even people and thought: *All hope is lost; they've made one too many bad decisions; there's no recovery from that.*

Maybe you've thought those things too.

Yet Jesus asks us to put on new lenses. That where others see a dead stump, we look for new life. When others would uproot and throw away, Christ calls us to dig in and nourish. When others would give up, Jesus nudges us to look to the potential, the possibilities, the fruitfulness that God brings.

Who in your life most feels like a dead stump right now?

Do you believe Christ can bring shoots of new life in that person? Why or why not?

It's worth noting that an olive tree can't thrive again on its own. Restoring an olive tree requires love and patience, hard work and close proximity.

Yet when an abandoned tree is nurtured and brought back to life from near-death, it comes to live with renewed energy. The shoots grow so fast, some say you can almost hear them.[6]

Who is the person God is calling you to nurture back to life?

What steps can you take to pour into this person and bring the renewing power of the Holy Spirit in their life?

CLOSING PRAYER

Ask God to equip you to help others flourish as you bring the healing presence of Christ wherever you go.

DAY FOUR: READ AND LEARN

Read chapter 8 of the *Taste and See* book, "The Perfect Ending to the Perfect Meal." Use the space below to note any insights or questions you want to share at the next group session.

What stood out to you most about Margaret's description of the Passover meal?

Mama Vered says, "They must know where they came from. This is our story from slavery to freedom." Why is this so important to the Jewish people? Why is this so important for followers of Jesus?

Relishing the Olive and Its Oil 113

Margaret writes, "In community, God touches our physical appetites and spiritual affections." How have you found this to be true in your life?

What steps do you need to take to begin your own adventure of tasting and seeing God's goodness?

 TASTE AND SEE EXPERIENCES

Choose one (or more) of the following activities to grow more intentional in your relationships with one other and God.

1. You can infuse your olive oil with your own flavors. Use lemon peel, oregano, basil, rosemary, garlic, or thyme (maybe even the spice you started growing from the Tasty Activity in session one). Add your spice to the oil and wait a few weeks. You can also speed up the process by placing the mixture on low heat for 5–8 minutes. These can usually be refrigerated for several weeks.

2. Think of one person in your community who may be on the margins or new to the area. Invite them to coffee or to share a meal together.

3. Pray over your home. If you've never prayed over your home, consider inviting your family members to join you. Pray over each room in your home and ask God to fill your home with his presence, love, and grace. Ask God to remove anything in the home that does not bring joy to him. As you move through the home, dab olive oil above each doorpost as a symbol of consecrating your home as holy and pure.

4. Select three healing stories of Jesus from the Gospels and read them back-to-back. What commonalities do you see among the stories? How are each of the people's lives transformed physically, spiritually, and emotionally? What do you need to do to experience God's deeper healing work in you?

Discovering the Liturgy of the Table

HOMEWORK GROUP DISCUSSION

Reflecting on all you've read in the *Taste and See* book and the homework you did in the Bible study guide, what stood out to you most?

GETTING STARTED (10–15 minutes)

TASTY ACTIVITY: A CELEBRATION OF THE GOODNESS OF GOD

What you'll need:
- Each person to bring food and a recipe to share
- Party balloons or fun decorations
- Digital camera or cell phone with camera

1. Decorate the room with balloons, streamers, wildflowers, and anything you can find to create a festive atmosphere.

2. Enjoy laughing, talking, sharing, and catching up as you eat together.

3. Invite participants to share what they've been learning through the *Taste and See* book and study guide homework.

4. Take a photo of your group and send it to hello@margaretfeinberg.com. We want to see your smiling faces!

5. Discuss the following:

- What activity could your group do together to help meet the needs of hunger within the community?

- Don't just talk about a possible activity—commit to helping others taste and see God's goodness in a tangible way. (Again, please share your stories with us at hello@margaretfeinberg.com.)

 PLAY SESSION 6 VIDEO (18 minutes)

NOTES

The Liturgy of the Table

Creator of all things delicious and nutritious,
May we come into each other's presence and
recognize that you are among us.
May we crack open the hurts behind our smiles and
have you feed the unspoken hungers deep within.
May you break down our walls as we break our bread.
May our hearts be filled as we fill our cups.
May those who gather here today taste from the
Bread of Life and drink from the Living Water.
May we glimpse the Garden of Eden that was
and the feast of the lamb to come.
May we taste and see your goodness,
not just in the food we eat,
but in the company we keep.
God, pull up a chair.
Eat with us today.
Amen.

You can have the most incredible tablescape and food spread, and it's incomplete without giving thanks.

We're such an abundant country that we don't know where food comes from and we waste 30 to 40 percent of what we have.

Gratitude shifts the focus from the "me" to the "we." It draws us outside of ourselves. *It leads us to action.*

When we give thanks, we can't just give thanks for the end product; we need to consider the whole process.

Gratitude is the best response *whenever* and *wherever* you taste and see God's goodness.

VIDEO DISCUSSION

1. What stood out to you most from today's teaching?

2. Margaret said, "Food can so easily become a commodity, a transaction, something we purchase and consume and toss out with little to no thought and little to no gratitude." How can you rethink your prayers around the table to reflect and express deeper gratitude?

3. Invite participants to read 1 Thessalonians 5:18 and Philippians 4:4. Take a moment to play The Gratitude Game—Bing! How does gratitude change you? The atmosphere in the room?

4. How do you think you will read the Bible differently after going through this study?

5. How has your understanding of God and his presence grown or deepened through this study?

6. How are you gathering around the table differently now that you've gone through this study?

7. What steps can you take to launch your own adventure of tasting and seeing God's goodness?

See Bible Memory Verse p. 125

CLOSING PRAYER

As you close in prayer, ask:
- God to expand each participant's capacity to taste and see God's goodness.
- The Holy Spirit to increase expectancy for Jesus at every meal.
- That each participant would experience Christ's presence during table time.

Memorization Flash Cards

Scripture memorization is a spiritual discipline useful to fill our minds with what our heart needs. Psalms 119:11 says, "I have hidden your word in my heart that I might not sin against you." When we memorize Scripture, it's easier to share the good news of Jesus, remain anchored in God's truth in difficult situations, and learn to meditate and delight in God's law (Psalm 1:2).

(cont.)

If you're like me, memorization doesn't always come easily. When spending time disciplining myself in Scripture memorization, I have to think of mnemonic games or tricks to get each verse or passage to stick. I encourage you to do the same. Here are a few helpful hints that may assist you as you memorize each session's verse(s):

- Choose a translation that is easiest for you to remember or one you are most familiar with.
- Practice by writing the verse three times. Challenge yourself to write it without looking.
- Spend time dissecting the verse and its meaning, using the surrounding verses and a commentary. Scripture memory is easier when the passage is fully understood.
- Read the verse aloud three times, and then try to recite it without looking.
- Use Google to see if any worship songs have been written about the passage you're memorizing. Or make up your own song to practice reciting.
- Find an accountability partner with whom you can recite verses together.
- Set a goal date to have a certain Scripture memorized.
- Write the Scripture on colorful pieces of paper or paint it on a canvas with your favorite Pinterest-y materials. Hang the artwork around your home or workplace to be reminded of the verse often.
- Write the individual words on different note cards, mix them up, and then try to put the words back in order.
- Be sure to break down the verse you're memorizing into smaller chunks to make them easier to swallow.

Don't get discouraged! Scripture memorization is a discipline that requires practice. I hope the flash cards provided here will be something you carry with you throughout this study as you begin the process of memorizing.

 **SESSION 1**

"When he was at table with them, he took the bread and blessed and broke it and gave it to them. And their eyes were opened, and they recognized him."

(LUKE 24:30 ESV)

 **SESSION 2**

"Everyone will sit under their own vine and under their own fig tree, and no one will make them afraid."

(MICAH 4:4 NIV)

 SESSION 3

"Watch out and beware of the leaven of the Pharisees and Sadducees."

(MATTHEW 16:6 NASB)

 SESSION 4

"Salt is good, but if it loses its saltiness, how can it be made salty again? It is fit neither for the soil nor for the manure pile; it is thrown out."

(LUKE 14:34–35 NIV)

 SESSION 5

"Jesus went out as usual to the Mount of Olives, and his disciples followed him. On reaching the place, he said to them, 'Pray that you will not fall into temptation.' He withdrew about a stone's throw beyond them, knelt down and prayed, 'Father, if you are willing, take this cup from me; yet not my will, but yours be done.'"

(LUKE 22:39–42 NIV)

 SESSION 6

"Taste and see that the Lord is good; blessed is the one who takes refuge in him."

(PSALM 34:8 NIV)

Leif's Honey Mustard Dressing

1 tablespoon mayonnaise
1 tablespoon honey
2 tablespoons yellow mustard
½ teaspoon white vinegar
Pinch of salt
Pinch of pepper

DIRECTIONS

Combine ingredients in small bowl until mixed. Refrigerate before and after serving. Makes 4–6 servings.

Roasted Figs and Brussels Sprouts

Brussels sprouts, trimmed and halved (approx. 2 cups)
1 small sweet onion, sliced
8 figs, quartered
1½ tablespoons olive oil
Leaves from 6 sprigs of thyme
Salt and pepper to taste
1 tablespoon aged balsamic vinegar

DIRECTIONS

1. Preheat oven to 400 degrees F.
2. Toss Brussels sprouts, onion, and figs with the olive oil and lay on a baking sheet lined with parchment paper. Sprinkle with thyme leaves, salt, and pepper.
3. Roast for about 25–30 minutes, turning the Brussels sprouts at least once to evenly roast.
4. Once the Brussels sprouts appear slightly shriveled, remove from the oven and toss with the aged balsamic vinegar. Cool slightly. Serves 2–3.

18-Minute Matzo

1 cup flour—half cup of barley and half cup of emmer, or favorite options including gluten

⅓ cup water

Parchment paper

DIRECTIONS

1. Preheat oven to 450.
2. Set timer to 18 minutes. Start timer the moment the flour and water meet.
3. Mix flour and water and add extra flour and water until mixture feels moist but not sticky.
4. Knead until smooth.
5. Divide into four pieces and roll out until flat.
6. Poke with fork in straight lines that are no further away than a quarter inch.
7. Place on parchment lined baking sheet.
8. Bake 4–5 minutes and remove from oven within 18-minute time frame.

Dark Chocolate Sea Salt Cookies (Gluten-free)

3 cups powdered sugar

¾ cup unsweetened dark chocolate cocoa powder

¼ teaspoon fine salt

½ teaspoon salt flakes

4 large egg whites at room temperature

2 teaspoons vanilla

Parchment paper

(Bonus ingredients: 2½ cups walnuts and 1 cup peanut butter chips)

DIRECTIONS

1. Preheat oven to 350. Line two baking sheets with parchment paper.
2. In a large bowl, mix powdered sugar, cocoa powder, and fine salt. Add egg whites and vanilla and whisk together until most clumps are gone. If you over-whisk, the batter will stiffen. Spoon onto baking sheet, making 22–24 cookies. Sprinkle a few salt flakes on the top of each cookie.

(cont. on back)

3. Bake cookies 15–18 minutes. Pull from oven when cookies are glossy, firm to the touch, and cracked on the surface.
4. Slide the parchment paper on two wire cooling racks. Use a spatula to loosen the cookies from the parchment paper shortly after they come out of the oven.

Bonus: Leif prefers to add 2½ cups of walnut halves and 1 cup of peanut butter chips to the recipe. We'll often bake our cookies side by side and when we share them, we'll ask people to vote between Team Margaret and Team Leif to decide which is best. We'd love to know your vote! If you try both recipes, email us at hello@margaretfeinberg.com and let us know which you prefer.

Fresh Italian Olive Oil Dip

2 cloves garlic, finely minced
1 tablespoon fresh oregano, minced
1 tablespoon fresh rosemary, minced
1 tablespoon fresh parsley, minced
2 teaspoon fresh basil, minced
1/4 teaspoon crushed red pepper flakes
1/2 teaspoon kosher salt
1/4 teaspoon ground black pepper
A squeeze of fresh lemon juice
Olive oil for serving

DIRECTIONS

1. Put first eight ingredients in a small food processor. Chop briefly until all herbs are about the same size.
2. Stir in lemon juice.
3. For every tablespoon of this mix, add two tablespoons of olive oil on a small plate.

The Liturgy of the Table

Creator of all things delicious and nutritious,

May we come into each other's presence and recognize that you are among us.

May we crack open the hurts behind our smiles and have you feed the unspoken hungers deep within.

May you break down our walls as we break our bread.

May our hearts be filled as we fill our cups.

May those who gather here today taste from the Bread of Life and drink from the Living Water.

May we glimpse the Garden of Eden that was and the feast of the lamb to come.

May we taste and see your goodness, not just in the food we eat, but in the company we keep.

God, pull up a chair. Eat with us today. Amen.

OLIVE TAPENADE

1 cup pitted Kalamata olives

2 teaspoons capers

1 teaspoon chopped garlic

2 teaspoons fresh thyme leaves, plus more for garnish

2 tablespoons olive oil

2 teaspoons balsamic vinegar

Kosher salt and freshly ground black pepper, to taste

Bread or crackers

DIRECTIONS

1. Pulse olives, capers, garlic, and thyme in a food processor until a coarse mixture forms. Add olive oil, balsamic, salt, and pepper, and pulse to combine.
2. Serve with your favorite cracker or a fresh piece of French baguette.

Notes

1. Wendell Berry, "The Gift of Good Land," in *The Gift of Good Land: Further Essays Cultural and Agricultural* (New York: North Point Press, 1981), 281.

2. Norman Wirzba, *Food and Faith: A Theology of Eating* (Cambridge: Cambridge University Press, 2011), 34.

3. https://www.sciencedaily.com/releases/2014/09/140922110149.htm.

4. Job 6:6 ESV.

5. Thanks to Mariam Feinberg Vamosh (not related) and her book *Food at the Time of the Bible: From Adam's Apple to the Last Supper* (Nashville: Abingdon, 2004), 74–77.

6. Mort Rosenblum, *Olives: The Life and Lore of a Noble Fruit* (New York: North Point, 1996), 31.

I am so delighted that we have the opportunity to Taste and See God's goodness together. In appreciation and celebration, I've put together some free gifts for you—including fun party invitations, posters, recipe cards, and bonus recipes. I'd love to send these to you for your surprise and delight. Simply email us at:

hello@margaretfeinberg.com

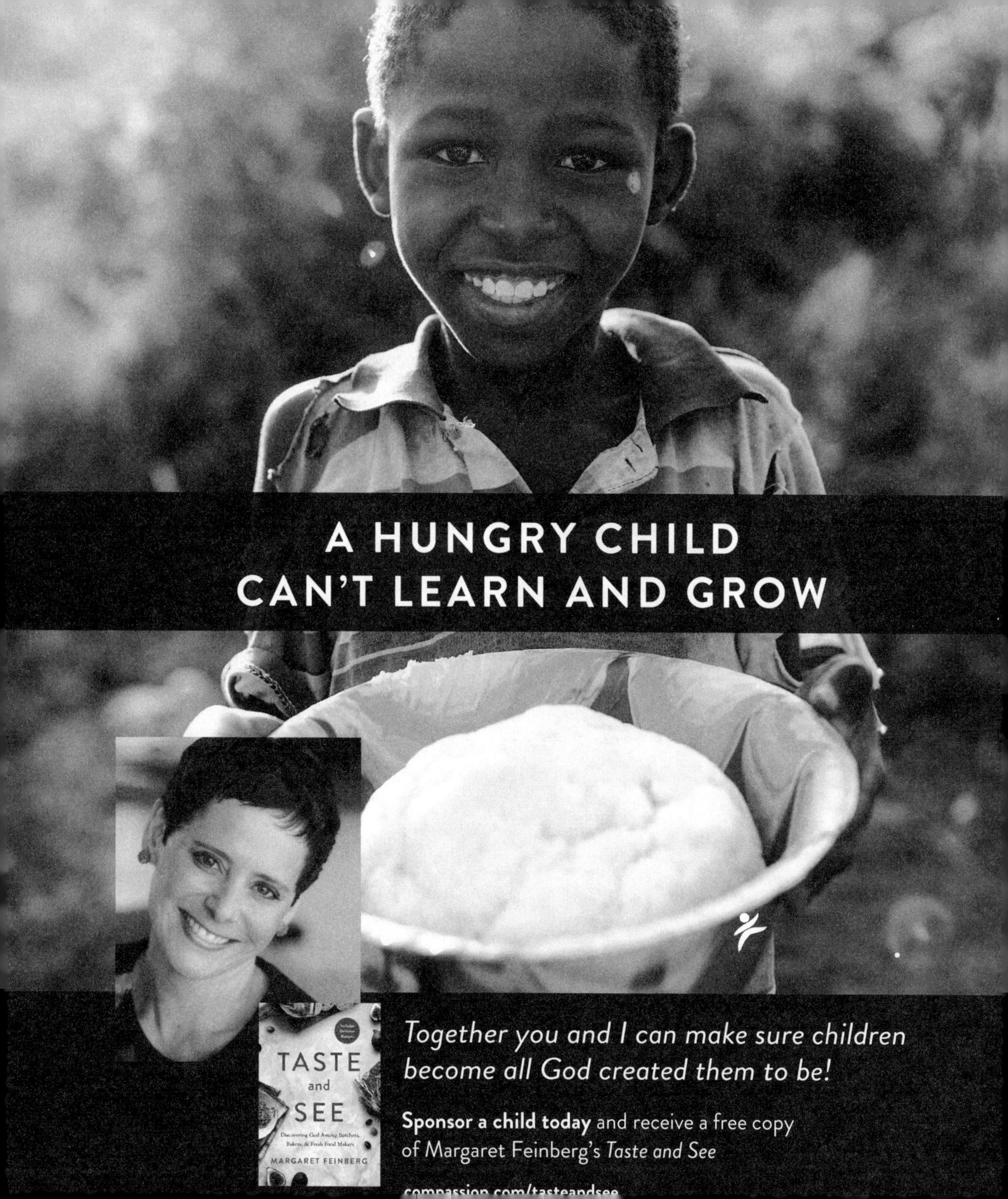
A HUNGRY CHILD
CAN'T LEARN AND GROW
TASTE
and
SEE
Discovering God Among Butchers, Bakers, & Fresh Food Makers
MARGARET FEINBERG
Together you and I can make sure children become all God created them to be!
Sponsor a child today and receive a free copy of Margaret Feinberg's Taste and See
compassion.com/tasteandsee

margaretfeinberg.com

Savor Life. Nourish Friendships. Embark on New Adventures.
at www.margaretfeinberg.com

On the site, you'll find:

- Weekly giveaways
- Free e-newsletter sign-up
- Margaret's personal blog
- Interactive discussion board

- Video an audio clips
- Secret sales and promotions
- Travel schedule
- Great prices on Bible studies

 become a fan on facebook
facebook.com/margaretfeinberg

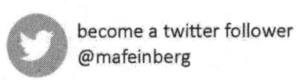 become a twitter follower
@mafeinberg

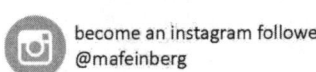 become an instagram follower
@mafeinberg

Taste and See

Discovering God among Butchers, Bakers, and Fresh Food Makers

Margaret Feinberg

God is a foodie who wants to transform your supper into sacrament.

One of America's most beloved teachers and writers, Margaret Feinberg, goes on a remarkable journey to unearth God's perspective on food. She writes that since the opening of creation, God, the Master Chef, seeds the world with pomegranates and passionfruit, beans and greens and tangerines. When the Israelites wander in the desert for forty years, God, the Pastry Chef, delivers the sweet bread of heaven. After arriving in the Promised Land, God reveals himself as Barbecue Master, delighting in meat sacrifices. Like his Foodie Father, Jesus throws the disciples an unforgettable two-course farewell supper to be repeated until his return.

This groundbreaking book provides a culinary exploration of Scripture. You'll descend 400 feet below ground into the frosty white caverns of a salt mine, fish on the Sea of Galilee, bake fresh matzo at Yale University, ferry to a remote island in Croatia to harvest olives, spend time with a Texas butcher known as "the Meat Apostle," and wander a California farm with one of the world's premier fig farmers.

With each visit, Margaret asks, "How do you read these Scriptures, not as theologians, but in light of what you do every day?" Their answers will forever change the way you read the Bible—and approach every meal.

Taste and See is a delicious read that includes dozens of recipes for those who, like Margaret, believe some of life's richest moments are spent savoring a meal with those you love.

Perhaps God's foodie focus is meant to do more than satisfy our bellies. It's meant to heal our souls, as we learn to taste and see the goodness of God together. After all, food is God's love made edible.

See you around the table!

Available in stores and online!

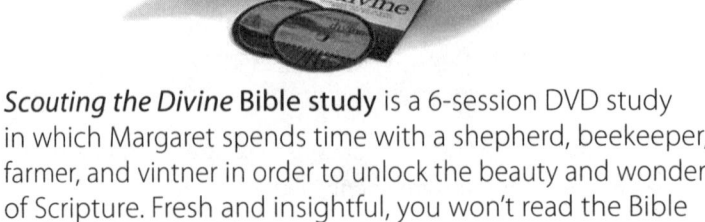

Scouting the Divine Bible study is a 6-session DVD study in which Margaret spends time with a shepherd, beekeeper, farmer, and vintner in order to unlock the beauty and wonder of Scripture. Fresh and insightful, you won't read the Bible the same way again.

To receive a FREE DVD sampler of *Scouting the Divine* and other DVD Bible studies, simply email **sampler@margaretfeinberg.com**. We'll get one in the mail to you.

Visit **margaretfeinberg.com/store** to order.

Pursuing God Study Guide
Encountering His Love and Beauty in the Bible

Margaret Feinberg

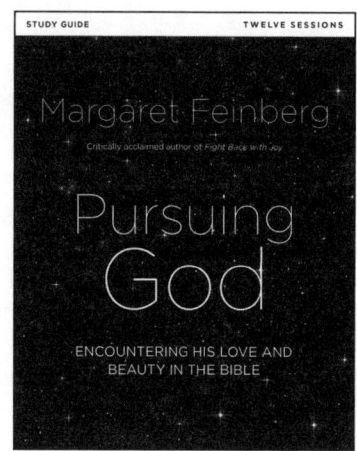

Genesis and the Gospel of John are written to spark your desire to pursue a deeper relationship with Jesus Christ. From the opening scene of God walking in the garden with humanity to Jesus hunched in prayer in the Garden of Gethsemane, this 12-week video Bible study (DVD/digital videos sold separately) will awaken you to the Lord's beauty and love in a fresh and transformative way.

This study guide includes ideas for group experiential activities and icebreakers, as well as between-sessions personal studies to dig deeper into Scripture on your own.

Sessions include:

1. Encountering God (Genesis 1–3)
2. Call on the Name of the Lord (Genesis 4–11)
3. The Pursuit, the Promise, and the Provision (Genesis 12–23)
4. When Love Goes Right and When Love Goes Wrong (Genesis 24–27)
5. It's Not about You (Genesis 28–36)
6. Finding God among Prisons and Palaces (Genesis 37–50)
7. Encountering Jesus (John 1–3)
8. When God Sees through You (John 4–8)
9. Recognizing the Blind Spots (John 9–11)
10. When Worship Costs More than Expected (John 12–17)
11. Mistakes that Refine Instead of Define (John 18–19)
12. The Hope and Healing of Resurrection (John 20–21)

Designed for use with the *Pursuing God Video Study* (sold separately). Previously published as *Pursuing God's Love Participant's Guide* and *Pursuing God's Beauty Participant's Guide*.

Available in stores and online!